COURBEE' EXOTICA

YOUR POWER IS CHOYCE

Unapologetically Plus & Unapologetically Sexy!

Courbee' (Courbe) is defined as "curvy" in French. Exotica means things that excitingly different or unusual. Curvy Beautiful Talent Plus Size Talent – Welcome to Courbee' Exotica Revolicion' Magazine June 2021 Issue.

There are over 14 billion plus size women (size 8 to 28) all over the world. Historically, we have been ignored, marginalized, teased, and out casted by society, social media, fashion designers, film producers, casting directors, advertisers, fashion industry and Hollywood.

We are excited to announce that Plus Size talent has arrived from the sets of Hollywood to the runways of New York, Milan, and Paris. Plus is a Choyce…. with *Choyce Comes Power!*

We have talent, beautiful models, singers, and actors who just happened to be Plus Size: Lizzo, Tamela Mann Libris, Crosse, Queen Latifah, Mo'Nique, Gabourey Sidbe, Rebel Wilson, Octavia Spencer, Melissa McCarthy, Oprah Winfrey, and so many more! #NoMore – Fat shaming, bullying, sexual assault, and the marginalization of Plus Size Talent!

In June's magazine we are excited to feature International Plus Size Model Claudia Floraunce – "Journey to Love." Also, in this issue there are photos and articles of Social Justice Black Life Matters – Fashion and Photographer: 1619 to 2019 The Insurrection and Black Vote, Photographer Joes Pagan of Jose Pagan Photography is debuting his Black Light Series, and Pictorials of the 20 sexiest Plus Size Models in the USA!

Remember,
Plus is Power and You Have a Choyce!
Always Share Love,
Jamila Jay

Jamila Jay
Editor in Chief
JamilacChoyce@ChoycePlusSizeModelsin.com
JamilaJayPlusSizeCasting.com

CONTENTS

COURBEE EXOTICA
REVILISION' MAGAZINE

JAMILA JAY, LOS ANGELES, CA
Dress Size 1 6 Height 5'9-

JAMILA JAY CHOYCE

LOS ANGELES, CA

www.JamilaJayPlusSizeCasting.com

JAI ,
Los Angeles,
California

Dress Size
14/16
Height 5'8

COLORS
ARE LOVE !

As a highly successful real estate investor for over seventeen years, Briggs is driven to obtain the highest standards for his clients. His successes as an effective motivational speaker and published author were developed from life experience. Through those exceptional skills, he learned the art of passive income. Chayo can assist his clients in procuring their prosperous future, breaking the chains of financial distress.

Chayo Briggs
website: chayobriggs.com

Credit is the New Money

"The desire for gold is not for gold. It is for the means of freedom and benefit." ~ Ralph Waldo Emerson~

What is credit? This is a common question asked by many people around the world. Society is becoming heavily dependent on credit for daily necessities; it's not just for buying a house or car anymore. The job market and pay scales play a large role in someone's financial well-being. Even the ability to gain employment or rent an apartment is determined by a credit resume, and the impact of being denied credit can place a heavy burden on one's future. It could mean the difference between a healthy lifestyle or living paycheck to paycheck; hoping nothing major happens that might cost someone their transportation or a place to live.

The initial step is requesting your complete, accurate credit report. Not all reports are the same, and not all are accurate. Annualcreditreport.com is a great suggestion. They are free to anyone once a year. Credit bureaus rely on third parties to report your financial behavior, so not every item is reported to all three consumer credit bureaus (Equifax, Experian, and TransUnion). In this situation, not all the errors will report on each report. Since you can't predict which credit report(s) a creditor will use to determine your credit risk, all three of your reports should be in good condition to prevent missing out on credit in the future.

The next step is deciding who will file the disputes. As with many things in life, credit repair is a process you can do yourself, or hire a professional. The option will depend on what your report shows. In other words, if the report has simple, straightforward corrections, such as spelling errors or outdated items, then filing yourself may be fast and easy. However, not all disputes are easy. It may be less stressful to hire an experienced credit repair company to act on your behalf. If the situation requires you to supply large amounts of evidence to back up the claim, you may want some help. There are some of our top-rated credit repair companies that have decades of experience helping consumers remove items from their credit reports. Or you can contact <u>Chayo Briggs</u>. One of the best resolutions anyone can make is improving your credit rating. What better way to start the New Year than get your credit in shape?

Here are three resolutions to kick-start your monetary goals:

Create a Budget (or Improve the One You Have): If you are like most Americans, you probably don't have a detailed budget. If you do, give yourself a big hand, because you are elite. In fact, two out of three of your friends are probably envious of your budgeting skills. Think about it; over 200 million Americans are admiring your budgeting prowess.

Improve Your Credit Utilization Ratio: Debt utilization explained. While not necessarily glamorous, your Credit Utilization Ratio is pretty straightforward: it's how much of your credit limit you're using. Imagine you have a single credit card with a limit of $100 and no other loans/debts. If you've got an outstanding bill of $90 for your credit card, you've used up 90 percent of your credit limit ($90 of the $100 available). Whether it's true or not, a bank would consider 90 percent utilization a high risk. It signals that you're not living within your means because you used up almost all of your available credit.

Chayo understands the key to success comes through life experience; for that reason, he assists clients in procuring their prosperous future; breaking the chains of financial distress. By maintaining a solid credit score or working to build a good credit profile you will improve the chances of qualifying for a loan. A stellar credit report shows potential lenders you are prone to repaying debt and have established financial responsibility.

As an author and public speaker, Chayo's books, especially *Your Credit Defines Your Creditability*, offer readers inspiration to help them learn the fundamentals of rebuilding their credit, as well as entrepreneurial and financial skills. For over seventeen years, Chayo's mission is to educate minority communities on the importance of having good credit in today's society. When someone can build a positive credit resume, they can easily obtain passive income to increase their financial investments.

Now, Chayo understands that everyone suffers money troubles at one point or another. The most important question is: do you know how to overcome the issues?

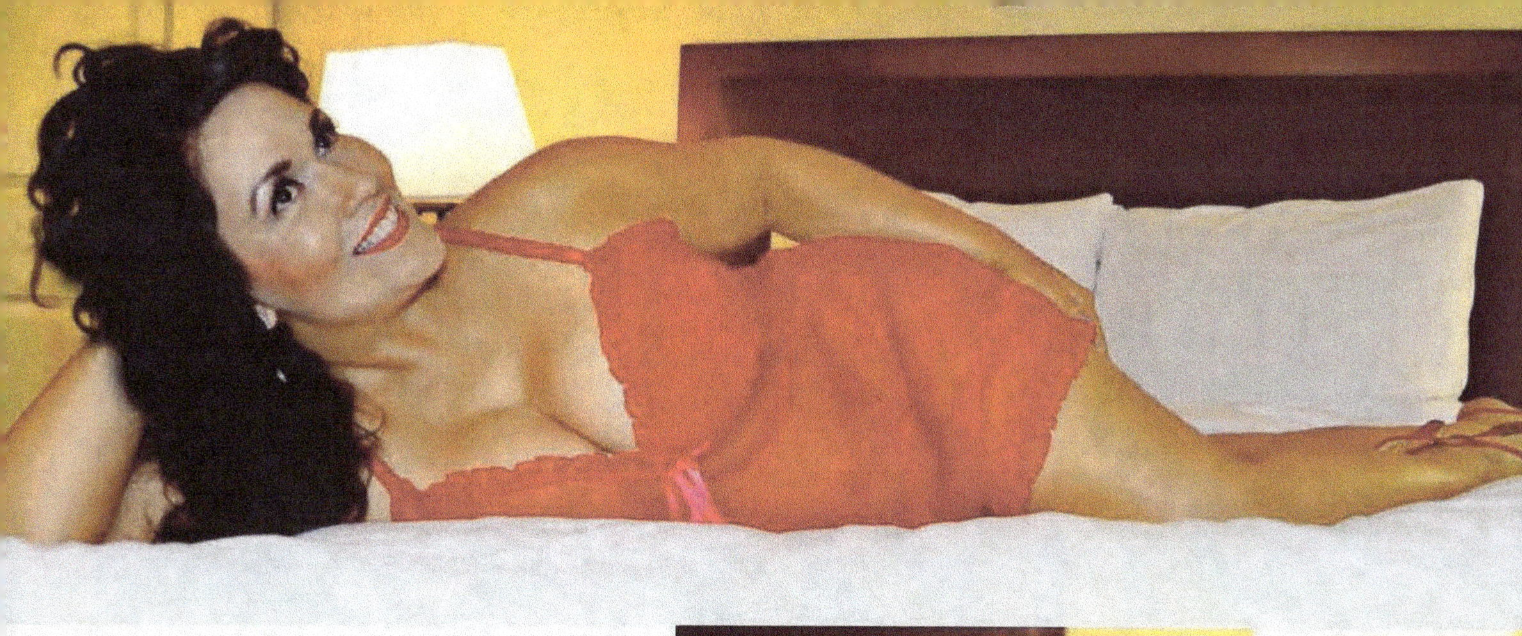

Mica
San Jose,
California
Dress Size
16/18
Height: 5'9

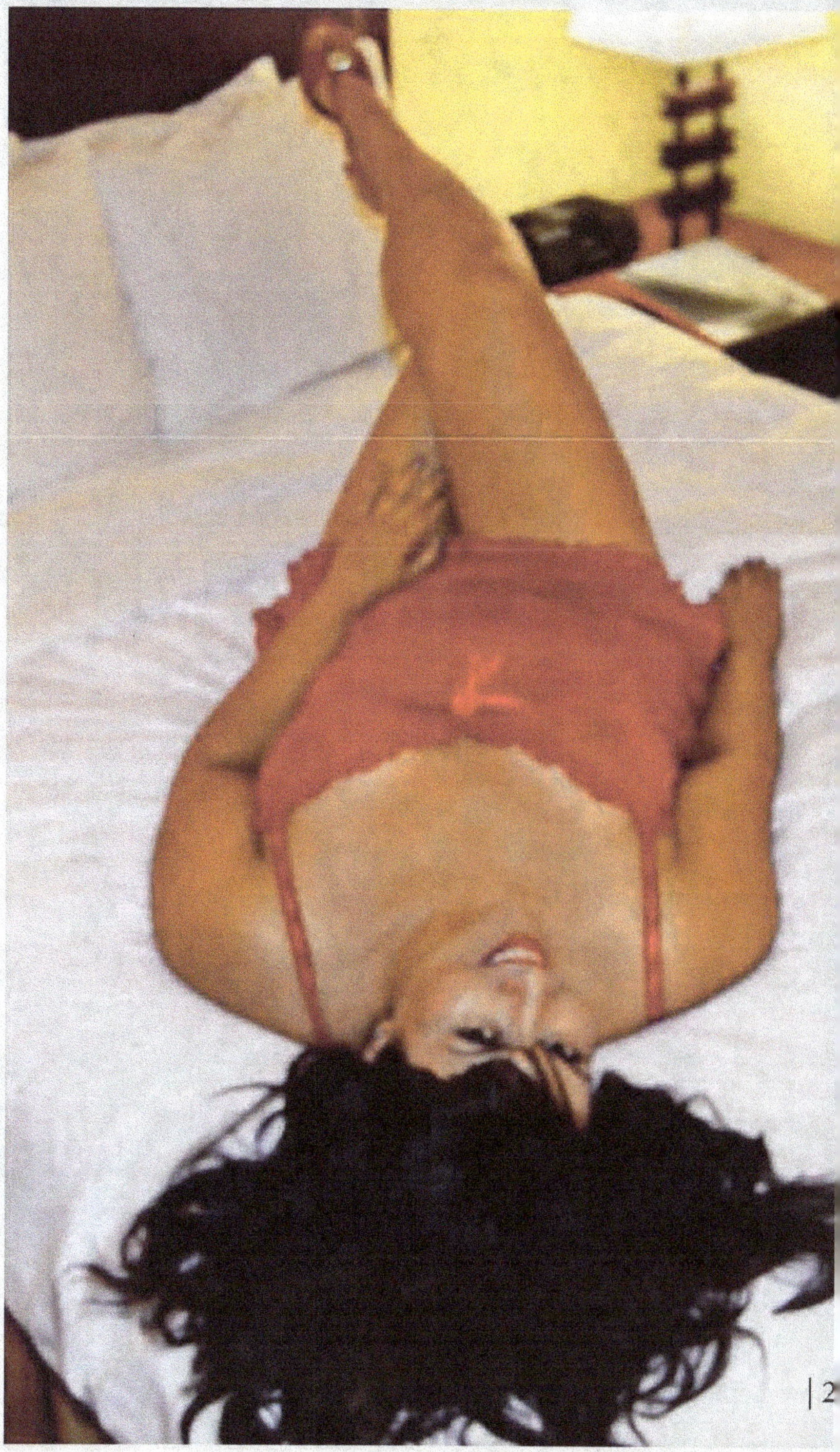

PHOTOTOUR
WITH
JOSE PAGAN
2021

Sponsored by

Livi Rae
LINGERIE

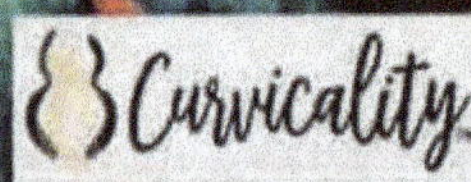
Curvicality

LACE

BELCANAJ COSMETICS

QUEEN
MAGAZINE

DIVAS PLUS MODEL

MSFM
Monique's School of Fashion & Modeling

Curvy

Blakk Media
DREAMS COME TRUE AT:
WWW.JOSEPAGANPHOTOGRAPHY.COM

Msster Mind of art & photography

Jose Pagan is a fashion and art photographer out of New York City but now based in the Tampa, Florida region. He is also a photographer that gives back to his community by lending his expertise to recognized charities such as Milagros Day Worldwide and Hunks4Hope. A product of the culturally rich Latino community of Washington Heights in Manhattan, he has used his creative mind to take the industry by storm with his eclectic art photography and fashion vision. He has a talent that garners a great deal of attention in today's high-end market.

IG@MODELASIAMONE
JOSE PAGAN PHOTOGRAPH

cece0618
JOSE PAGAN PHOTOGRAPHY

IAM.REAL_KATERIMARIE
Jose Pagan Photography

IAMLISARACHEL
JOSE PAGAN PHOTOGRAPHY

IG@MODELASIAMONET
JOSE PAGAN PHOTOGRAPHY

JOSE PAGÁN
JOSE PAGAN PHOTOGRAPHY

BEYOND THE BLACK LIGHT
"Curvangerous Blacklight Series"

Many in the fashion industry have noticed Jose Pagan's artistic eye. Soon after his initial exposure with his art projects, Jose has been hired by businesses and organizations to translate their visions. Jose first started out being hand-picked as East coast lead photographer for Designer Original, shooting several covers and many high-end editorials. Since then the magazine world fell in love with Jose's work. He has been published Elle UK, Harpers Bazaar UK, Elle Brazil, Heart & Soul magazine. The Plus industry also has welcomed Jose with open arms, and in doing so he has shot three covers for FabUplus and Plus Model magazine and countless others. Jose also was tapped as Director of Photography for Moda Mantra magazine. Yet again giving Jose the opportunity to flex his artistic eye in a medium that focuses strictly on modest fashion.

1. What inspired you to compose photos in the Black Light Series?

The Blacklight series was a natural evolution in my artistic journey. I love my wife and I love her body, now combine the fact that I love to bend the rules of art and create things that people haven't experienced I decided to go down this endless rabbit hole of surrealism. I loved the fact that to create the images you see in that series I had to work extremely hard to achieve those results. I felt for my work to have more substance I had to make sure the process was as close to science as it was to my infinite artistic vision. I didn't want to do easy art projects. Even this process made evolutionary jumps. I started venturing into art with emotional purpose as opposed to projects of vanity. I mean yeah, cool art with cool colors are fun but I yearned for more. I wanted my muse to connect with the viewers on an emotional level. It was important to convey to the audience a story that inspires the human experience on a new level. So yeah, my wife's naked body was a major catalyst for this amazing journey and till this day she still sits for my when I need to test out new props or techniques!

2. How did you choose the models, clothes, and makeup?

It's funny you ask because people always ask me how I get people to get naked? I have no clue myself because when I first started the project, I just started using everyday folk to be part of this project. When I was a cop, most of my muses were other cops who believed in my vision. Till this day most of my subjects and clients who do take part in the Blacklight sessions are people who never shot nude. My selection of participants for this series is organic. When I meet someone new, I gauge their aura. I get to know them and just bluntly ask them if they would be interested in doing art. 99% of the time the person is the free spirit I figured them to be. Now when it comes to props, clothing or makeup that too is organic. I would ask them about things in their life that may guide my vision and how to approach their session. Sometimes makeup is ad hoc and schemes are created on set as the shoot progresses. I do love to create sets when feasible. I enjoy the process of creating environments that add to the overall image.

Jose Pagán
Jose Pagan Photography

Beyond the Black Light
"Curvangerous Blacklight Series!"

3. Each model has a complete and unique concept, how did you come up with each concept?

As I research my muse, I find facts about them that lead to concepts. A recent client told me that she wanted to feel regal, so with that I created a headpiece that conveyed that royal message to the viewer. Sometimes I would also draw concepts on paper and store them until the right person for that vison came along. I've even created props and put it on my shelf for two year and then voila, a person came along and they matched perfectly. I try not to rush concepts or push them on clients if they do not fit. I love for everything to flow and tell a story, and if it takes me two weeks to create that concept I think it's well worth it.

4. What motivates your photography (Black Light and other images)?

I believe after years of photographing people for art, I get an emotional and spiritual rise from helping people level up. Getting naked in front of someone is not easy, but I believe once a person breaks that membrane of anxiety they go on to another level of confidence. I believe breaking through this level helps them in other aspects of their lives. What I aim in my sessions is not just to take a picture, but to give my clients an experience that lasts a lifetime.

THE ESSENCE OF A WOMAN'S SOUL
IS HER BODY!

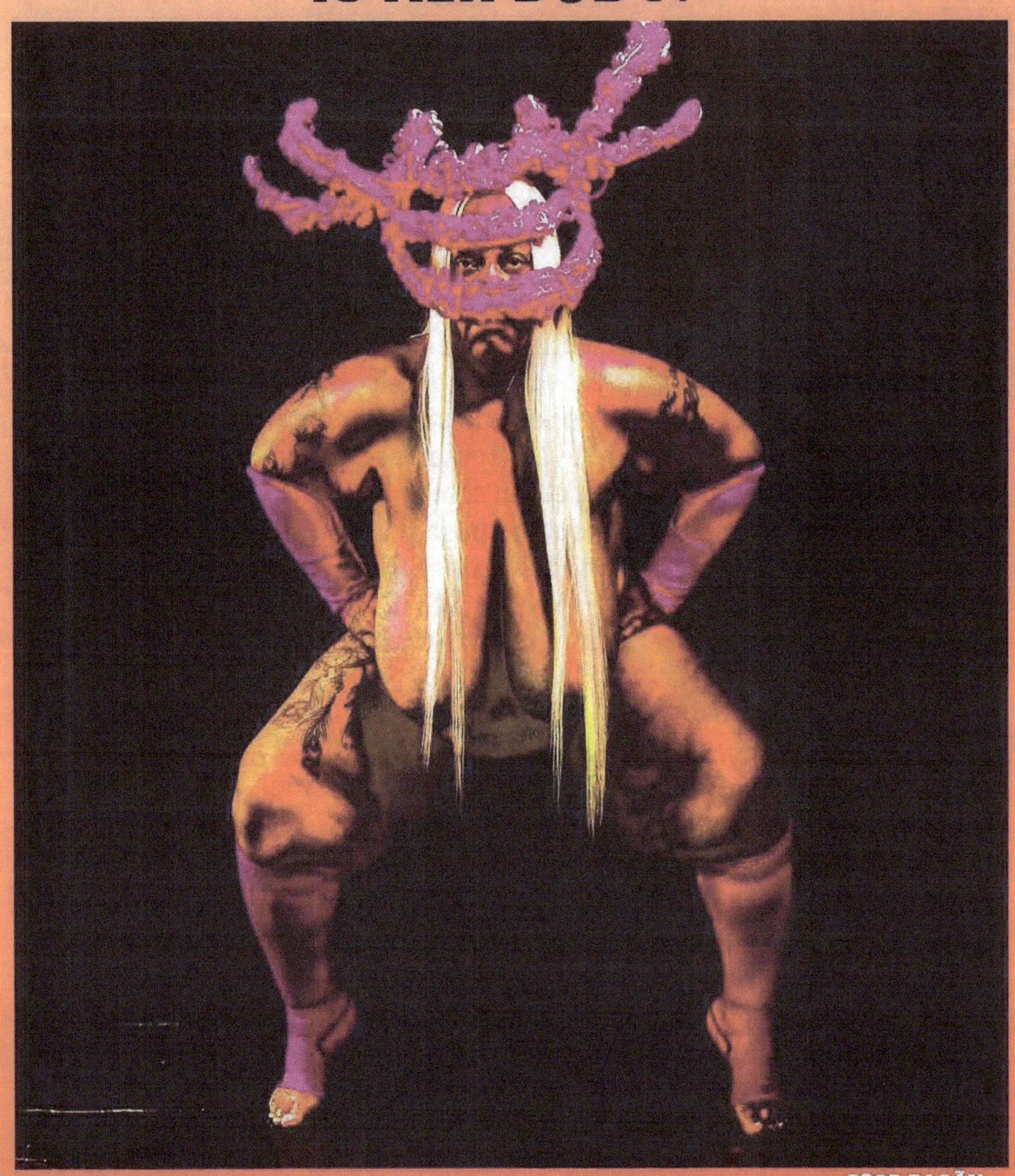

FB@IAMIRISPEREZ
a mister piece from the "master mind!"
IRIS PEREZ
JOSE PAGÁN
JOSE PAGAN PHOTOGRAPHYT

my body is art

ASHLEY RENEE

JOSE PAGÁN
JOSE PAGAN PHOTOGRAPHYT

IG@cakeladytressa
art, body, soul
VONTRESSA SALTER
Jose Pagán
JOSE PAGAN PHOTOGRAPHY

IG@IAMIRISPEREZ
this is magic!
IRIS PEREZ
Jose Pagán
JOSE PAGAN PHOTOGRAPHY

IG@kurve_dynasty

the muse, the model, the me!

Tonia Clincy

Jose Pagán
JOSE PAGAN PHOTOGRAPHY

the muse, the model, the m
TONIA CLINCY
Jose Pagán
JOSE PAGAN PHOTOGRAPHY

CARMELSASSY

Height
5'8
Dress Size
12/14
'Since the age of two, I
had a passion for
singing running thru
my veins.

As I got older, I
sang in the church
chior and started
to write poems
that eventually
turned into songs.

I am versatile and
open to any Genre
with three
different octaves
of my voice.'

Sacramento, CA

WWW.MKIPHOTOGRAPHER.COM

BOOK REVIEW

SINCE THE RAHA SERIES BEGAN, IT BLOSSOMED INTO SOMETHING INCREDIBLE. RAHA HAD CREATED SUCH INTENSE SENSATIONS IN ALBORZ, IT BECAME IMPOSSIBLE FOR HIM TO IMAGINE LIVING WITHOUT THE LOVE OF HIS LIFE.

"JIBY - SEXY LOVE MAKING"

In March 2020, when the pandemic spread across the world, everyone was locked
down for extended periods. The separation left Alborz's heart longing for his Eshghan
Once sanctions were lifted and leaving to travel the world once again, Alborz shared h
escapades in Jiby Sexy Love Making with his Raha.

On the 6th of September, 2020, Alborz finally met with Raha once again. During 2020,
they had only met once right before the lockdown.

Alborz stated, "By the time I finished writing Jiby Sexy Love Making at the end of March
2021, Raha and I had met again for 15 Jiby Sexy Love Making from 21st February 202
until 7th, March 2021. The indulgence with Raha has led me to write, 15 Sexy Love
Making Holidays.

Alborz and Raha find a passionate desire for each other in Jiby Sexy Love Making, whi
made them realize they were made for each other no matter what happened. The
pandemic brought forth moments that unfolded in greater love, more connection, an
passion for each other.

The Jiby Sexy Love Making allowed Raha to enjoy the feeling of power and control she
had over Alborz during sexy lovemaking, as she effortlessly brought wave after wave
pleasure, which made him utterly sexually obsessed with only Raha. Especially... on to
with chocolate syrup.

ACHIEVE YOUR DREAMS
We did, so can you!
You Have a Choyce
SHARE LOVE!
www.JamilaJayPlusSizeCasting.com
www.ChoyceTV.com
www. JamilaJayFashions.com

"FASHIONISTA
IS FOR
EVERYONE!
I RESPECT
VOGUE AND
FASHION!"
I AM...
SHAY REESE G

SHAI REESE 6
WASHINGTON, DC

L. Llewellyn James

In that capacity, Mr. James works as a Traditional Illustrator, Graphic Designer, 3d Computer Modeling Artist, Documentary Filmmaker and Voice-over Artist.

Mr. James has worked for an eclectic array of clientele, ranging from The Evangelical Lutheran Church in America, The Discovery Museum and Science Planetarium and The African-American Historical Association of Fairfield County, Connecticut.

You can see much more of Mr. James' work as a Filmmaker, Illustrator, Graphic Designer and 3d Computer Modeler via his website at www.alphamediaworks.com

His IG handle is @l_llewellyn_james, while he can be reached on Twitter @AlphaholicOne

Andre'tta Garnes

**THE QUINESSTENTIALENTERTAINER, =
ATLANTA, GEORGIA
Height 5'9 = Dress Size 20-22**

Michelle Woods-SSMC Rabidus Films LLC

"BEING BEAUTIFUL ME"

Andrétta Garnes – The Quinesstential Entertainer

George
Floyd
Lives
Forever
BLACK LIVES MATTER
PHILANDO CASTILE
BLACK
SAY THEIR
NAMES
MATTER
GEORGE
IN MEMORY OF
ERIC GARNER
PAINTED BY PITTSBURGH POLICE OFFICER
IN MEM
OF
WALTER
TRAYVON
STEPHON CLARK
SANDRA
BLAND
DIVISION

Black Lives Matter Movement

from a #HASTAG to A Global Movement

July 2013, George Zimmerman was acquitted for the shooting death of Travon Martin, a 17-year-old Black boy who had been walking in his father's Florida neighborhood. The pain, the hurt, and the blatant loss of life of a 17-year Black son, brother, cousin, and grandson resonated with Black, Brown, and White people all around the world.

Many folks took a paused and asked, "Does a Black life really matter? Who really cares about Black and Brown people in America and around the world?" I answered, "Yes, my live matters and so does my sons, brothers, cousins, nephew, and friends."

July 13 2013, was another important day. On that very same evening of the verdict announcement, Alicia Garza and some friends gathered for drinks. None of them thought Zimmerman would be acquitted on all charges. It's been nearly 8 years since the group formed after George Zimmerman's acquittal in the killing of Martin.

Alicia Garza, an Oakland activist, posted what she called a love letter to Black people on Facebook, telling them, "Our lives matter." Los Angeles activist Cullors turned it into a hashtag: #BlackLivesMatter. New York activist Opal Tometi built the digital platform. A few days later, Cullors called her friend Abdullah and 30 others together to form the first chapter of 16 chapters across North America.

Black Lives Matter is one of the most well-known organizations fighting for the well-being of Black people.

In 2012, the BLM movement was only a social media hashtag, #BlackLivesMatter, with three female Black organizers, Alicia Garza, Patrisse Cullors, and Opal Tometi. It created a Black-centered political will and movement building project called Black Lives Matter (BLM).

The phrase "Black Lives Matter" is being used now as more than just a hashtag -- it's a rallying cry.

At protests, it's what many demonstrators write on their signs or chant as they march. Online, it's what many have used to spread the message against police brutality. And globally, it's being used by many to show solidarity with Black people.

In 2014, the movement grew nationally and so did the unjust murder of Black people. After the deaths of Michael Brown in Missouri and Eric Garner in New York. Since then it has established itself as a worldwide movement, particularly after the death of George Floyd at the hands of police in Minneapolis,

MN. Most recently, #Black Lives Matter has spearheaded demonstrations worldwide protesting police brutality and systematic racism that overwhelmingly effects the Black community.

Momentum around the movement has grown amid calls for justice following the deaths of Ahmaud Arbery, Breonna Taylor and George Floyd.

While many believe the movement is more accepted than it once was, others remain skeptical of what it accomplishes and question its impact.

Here's what you need to know about the evolution of the movement, and why it matters.

STUDIES SHOW that the progress is slow:

Segregation, leaving majority Black communities behind. BLM's goal, according to its website, is to eradicate anti-Blackness and create a society where Black people are able to thrive in the US.

"We live in a country built to keep us away from these resources that we need," said Kailee Scales, managing director of the Black Lives Matter Global Network Foundation.

Police officers are almost four times as likely to use force on Black people than White people. Black people are also jailed at a disproportionate rate. Black Americans have lower access to health care and lack the same access to quality education.

"Folks in the movement have been consistently fighting to reverse that trend, to raise awareness that this is not the way we're supposed to live," Scales told CNN.

Since the hashtag launched, the organization has become more formalized, taken on specific branding and branched out into nationwide chapters -- all in an attempt to solidify the group and allow them to create national campaigns while engaging the broader community.

Organizers put together a website, which led to the development of local chapters of BLM, first in Los Angeles in 2013 and then throughout the country.

BLM Foundation, Inc is a global organization in the US, UK, and Canada, whose mission is to eradicate white supremacy and build local power to intervene in violence inflicted on Black communities by the state and vigilantes. By combating and countering acts of violence, creating space for Black imagination and innovation, and centering Black joy, we are winning immediate improvements in our lives."

Black Lives Matter has morphed into a global phenomenon, with ultra-active chapters throughout the United States, Canada and the United Kingdom. There's a strong international following and support in Australia, Denmark, France, Germany, and Japan.

NO JUSTICE NO PEACE
JUSTICE FOR PHILANDO CASTILE
RICE
IN MEMORY OF ERIC GARNER
BLACK LIVES MATTER
"SAY THEIR NAMES"
BLACK LIVES MATTER
TRAYVON
OSCAR
CAN'T BREATHE
BLACK LIVES MATTER
IN MEMORY OF ERIC GARNER
By PITTSBURGH POLICE OFFICER ALPHONSO SLOAN
THEY MADE ARRES BECAU WE SAW TH VIDEO
GEORGE FLOYD
STEPHON CLARK
SAND BLA
LOVING MEMORY OF BOTHAM JEAN

The Insurrection & the Black Vote

The Black Vote History, Historically, the founding fathers give the right to vote "to only land-owning white men." In 1776, New Jersey give the right to vote every who lived in the state, but quickly changed the law to exclude Blacks and Women. In 1965, white women were afforded the right to vote. During the 1950s and 60s, civil rights, anti-war, equality and voting rights for all became the for front of the movement. The Voting Act of 1965, outlawed voter's suppression. The act gave Blacks, women, Native Americans, and immigrants the legal right to vote.

However, in 2013, a Supreme Court, gutted the Voting Rights Acts. They eliminated key provisions that required federal oversight of districts based on their histories of voter discrimination.

The number of Black Americans eligible to vote for president has reached a record 30 million in 2020, with more than one-third living in nine of the nation's most competitive states – Arizona, Florida, Georgia, Iowa, Michigan, North Carolina, Ohio, Pennsylvania and Wisconsin – a higher share than the 29% of *all* U.S. eligible voters who live in these states. Nationwide, Black eligible voters now make up 12.5% of the U.S. electorate, up from 11.5% in 2000.

For many years, Black voters were the largest non-White racial or ethnic segment of the country's electorate, but for the first time in a presidential election they will be outnumbered by Hispanic eligible voters, at 32 million.

Georgia & the Black Vote, Georgia made history electing its first Black U.S. senator, Reverend Raphael Warnock. This was a victory decade in the making, organized Stacy Abrams. After losing the 2018, gubernatorial race, she strategized and organized to protect the voting rights of minorities. She delivered Georgia to the Democrats in the 2020 election as well as the Senate in January run-offs.

Trump told Georgia's Republican Secretary of State Brad Raffensperger in a now-infamous telephone call he needed a few thousand votes in Georgia, enough to help him win the 2020 US presidential election. "Look, all I want to do is this. I just want o find 11,780 votes, which is one more than we have, because we won the state."

Former President Donald Trump tried to disqualify the Black Vote not only in Georgia but in ot Pennsylvania, Arizona, and Illinois. They were the battleground states that Trump's campaigned filed unsuccessful lawsuits alleging voter fraud.

Philadelphia & the Black Vote In Philadelphia, the **Black voter** turnout defined the outcome of the election. Black Americans were disproportionately impacted by pandemic-related losses like work and health care, which many predicted would incentivize voting. The Philadelphia City Commissioners Office, which oversees elections, reported on their website that Philadelphia voter turnout is currently at 51.4%.

The erroneous claims of fraud were unfounded. On election night, Trump appeared to have a strong "lead" in Pennsylvania, and he expressed confidence he would win the state. He even wrongly "claimed" Pennsylvania's Electoral College votes in a tweet before the race had been decided. But in the days ahead, as more mail ballots were processed and counted, Joe Biden pulled ahead and ultimately won the state by 81,000 votes, or about 1%. The slow counting of mail ballots, and the way it eroded Trump's early advantage, was the direct and expected result of Pennsylvania's election rules — not fraud.

One of Trump's most frequent complaints is that Republicans weren't allowed to watch Pennsylvania's largest cities count votes. Trump has said observers were barred from even entering the facilities where votes were being counted.

That's not true. And in every county where Republicans raised objections, courts found that officials applied the observation rules evenly to both parties.

Arizona & the Black Vote In Arizona, the get-out-the-vote effort in Arizona translated into record-high turnout for African Americans, who helped deliver a win for Joe Biden in this traditionally conservative state and elected several Black candidates or almost did in state and local races. A Black Democratic State Rep. Reginald Bolding won reelection, said 60% of Arizona's Black registered voters cast ballots. A collective of progressive community and advocacy organizations led by people of color. The U.S. Census Bureau says Black voter turnout in the state was 44.2% in 2012 and 46.6% in 2016.

President Donald Trump is now claiming that an inspection of 100 ballots in Arizona showed he might have won the state by 90,000 votes. A lawsuit was filed, this one a federal action claiming "massive election fraud" in Arizona.

Former president laid the foundation for the insurrectionists which consisted a culmination of white supremacists: the Proud Boys, the Forever Trumpeters, police officers, QAnon, Oath Keeper, Three Percenters, and other far right militia groups. The rhetoric fed to them by former president that the "election was rigged," massive voter's fraud, and question the legality of legally cast ballots insinuated a civil war!

On January 6, 2021, an army of white supremacists "stormed" the U.S. Capitol building in Washington, D.C. Inside the building, a joint session of the United States Congress was convened to certifying the tally of the recent U.S. presidential election. The results of the election were submitted to Congress by the Electoral College, itself a constitutionally sanctioned body that endured withering criticism for certifying the election results tallied by the fifty independent states in the 2020 presidential election.

About an hour before "breaching" the Capitol ground's outer perimeter, a mob attended a rally on the Ellipse near the White House. The rally was headlined by former president Donald Trump. Trump amplified yet again the meritless claims that the presidential election of 2020 had been "stolen and rigged" from him and his supporters. More than sixty lawsuits challenging the integrity of the results filed by the incumbent President's legal teams and allies all failed. A number of these lawsuits were decided by circuit court judges who Trump himself appointed.

Trump's lawyers have defended his speeches and tweets leading up to the Jan. 6, Capitol riots as protected by his First Amendment right to free speech. But during his second impeachment trial the *House Managers* prosecuting him focused on what Trump didn't say as the riot escalated. They assert Trump's muted response supports their case of inciting insurrection – the charge against the former president in his second impeachment trial.

"We were looking for Nancy to shoot her in the friggin' brain but we didn't find her." They were referring to the House Speaker Nancy Pelosi (D.-Calif.) Pelosi is the only woman in U.S. history to serve as speaker. She is second in the presidential line of succession, after vice president Kamala Harris. Federal authorities are attributing those words to insurrectionist's Dawn Bancroft. Bancroft and Diana Santos-Smith are now facing charges over the January 6 riot at the U.S. Capitol.

BRELEE

"A strong woman looks a challenge dead in the eye and gives it a wink." #breleeng

AUSTIN ,TEXAS

DRESS SIZE: 24
HEIGHT: 5'4
BUST: 44
CUP: DDD
HIPS: 51
WAIST: 39

MY JOURNEY TO LOVE

ou deserve
elationship
here both
sides
ever stop
trying.

If only you
knew
how much
I think
about you.
goodlifequoteru.com

m selfish.
want you
myself,
can't help

I AM IN LOVE WITH ME!

MY HIPS, THIGHS, STOMACH LEGS, LOVE HANDLE, & EVERYTHING ELSE!

I LOVE ME WITH ALL MY HEART, BODY, & SOUL!

IF YOU'RE NOT HAPPY ABOUT HOW YOU LOOK, YOU HAVE TO QUESTION HOW MUCH SELF-LOVE YOU HAVE.

I LOVE MYSELF

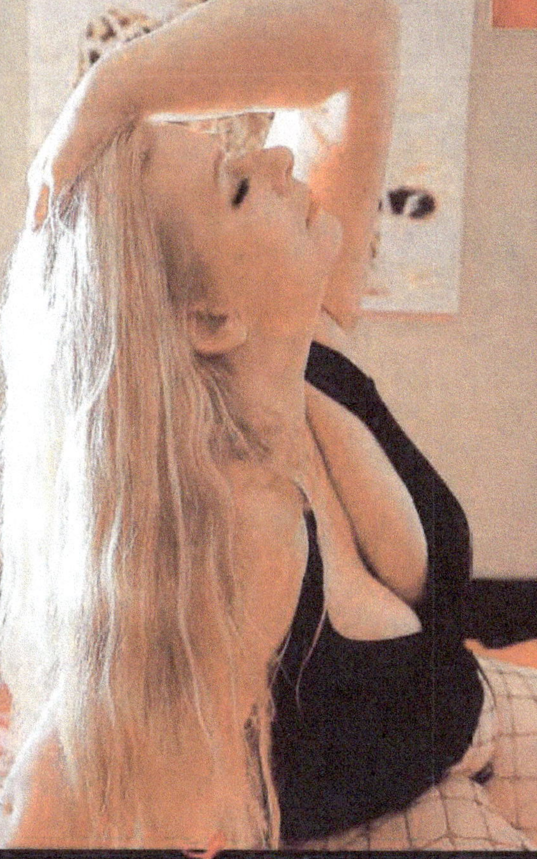

Love
Claudia

IG @ClaudiaFlourance

Roxanne Monroe, Los Angeles, California

Dress size 18/20
Height 5'10
Shoe size 11

TYE LOVE, Height 5'3. Dress Size 8-14
Sacramento, CA

JACQELINE MIGLIORIE DAVIS

LAS VEGAS, NEVADA

HEIGHT 5'9 DRESS SIZE 18/20

In the last 5 years, I have obtained many success and overcame obstacles using my curvy healthier figure, finally to my advantage in a business that is friendlier to my smaller counterparts.

I have been published in numerous magazines, obtained several speaking roles as a supporting actress, two music videos, and countless extra roles.

I am a BRAND AMBASSADOR for several online companies, with my newest paid partnership with Adam and Eve Lingerie.

I have been recognized by big names such as Lane Bryant and Torrid.

My goals is to encourage women of all sizes and ages to believe in a body positive image. And keep grind no matter what life throws at you. I aspire to bring women together, be uplifting and helpful towards obtaining their goals, whatever they may be.

"I would love to embrace all of beautiful full figure sisters and show them that we can work together and not against each other.. let's win together!"
CRYSTAL
HEIGHT 5'2
DRESS SIZE
18/20

**PHILADELPHIA,
PENNSYLVANIA**

MY GOAL IS TO BECOME A SUCCESSFUL BUSINESS WOMAN. I HOPE TO INSPIRE OTHER FULL FIGURED WOMEN TO FOLLOW THEIR DREAMS WHATEVER IT MAY BE. I HOPE TO SHOW THEM THAT THEY ARE BEAUTIFUL NO MATTER THE SKIN THEY'RE IN.

I'VE LEARNED ON MY JOURNEY THAT SELF-CARE IS VERY IMPORTANT. MODELING IS SOMETHING THAT I ENJOY DOING WITHOUT EFFORT. I LIKE TO LOOK BEAUTIFUL AND I ENJOY DRESSING UP. I HOPE TO BECOME A SPEAKER FOR TEENAGE AND YOUNG ADULT WOMEN. WHO HAS BECOME A MOTHER AT AN EARLY AGE.

I BECAME A MOTHER AT AN EARLY AGE AND I WOULD LOVE TO SHARE MY STORY WITH OTHERS. MAYBE I CAN BE OF SOME HELP WITH THE TRIALS AND TRIBULATIONS OF BEING A TEEN MOM. MY ACHIEVEMENTS IN LIFE THAT I'M VERY PROUD OF ONE I ACHIEVED THE COURAGE TO TAKE TIME TO DO WHAT I REALLY LIKE

WHILE PURSUING MY MODELING CAREER THE SECOND THING WAS TO DO MY PHOTO SHOOT.

I STEPPED OUTSIDE OF THE BOX AND I DID A PHOTOSHOOT SOMEWHERE NEW AND THAT WAS A BIG ACHIEVEMENT FOR ME. ANOTHER GOAL THAT I FORGOT TO MENTION IS I REALLY WILL LOVE FOR ALL FULL FIGURE TO COME TOGETHER AND UNITE WE DON'T HAVE TO BE JEALOUS OR ENVIOUS OF EACH OTHER BUT TO EMBRACE EACH OTHER INDIVIDUALITY AND DIFFERENCE WE ARE ALL BEAUTIFUL AND BEAUTIFULLY AND WONDERFULLY MADE IN GOD'S EYES HE IS OUR CREATOR.

Plus Size Entreprenuer

Schanaque Watson
aka the "Real Coco Mocho"

My name is Schanaque Watson and I am 30 years old from Memphis Tennessee. I attended The University of Memphis where I obtained a Degree in Criminal Justice and Criminology along with two Minors in English and African and African American Studies. I also attended Strayer University where I obtained a Masters of Public Administration.

I have worked as a Mental Health Case Manager, Medical Social Worker, Probation Officer, Counselor in the Jail, and a Criminal Justice Case Manager. Working in the Criminal Justice Field has been such an eye opener, especially if you are a person to pass judgement. You definitely learn how to always have an unbiased opinion.

Modeling was something that truly came out of nowhere. After, experiencing a miscarriage in 2018, life just hit different. I gained so much weight and just no longer felt beautiful. At this point I started talking to God, and just asking him to guide and order my steps.

SCHANAQUE
WATSON

I HAVE WORKED AS A MENTAL HEALTH CASE MANAGER, MEDICAL SOCIAL WORKER, PROBATION OFFICER, COUNSELOR IN THE JAIL, AND A CRIMINAL JUSTICE CASE MANAGER. WORKING IN THE CRIMINAL JUSTICE FIELD HAS BEEN SUCH AN EYE OPENER, ESPECIALLY IF YOU ARE A PERSON TO PASS JUDGEMENT. YOU DEFINITELY LEARN HOW TO ALWAYS HAVE AN UNBIASED OPINION.

MODELING WAS SOMETHING THAT TRULY CAME OUT OF NOWHERE. AFTER, EXPERIENCING A MISCARRIAGE IN 2018, LIFE JUST HIT DIFFERENT. I GAINED SO MUCH WEIGHT AND JUST NO LONGER FELT BEAUTIFUL. AT THIS POINT I STARTED TALKING TO GOD, AND JUST ASKING HIM TO GUIDE AND ORDER MY STEPS. HE DEFINITELY DID! I STARTED DOING SEVERAL PHOTO SHOOTS AND JUST LOVED THE SPACE I WAS IN. AT THIS TIME I STARTED ENCOURAGING OTHER WOMEN TO EMBRACE EVERYTHING THROUGH EVERY OBSTACLE. WE ALL HAVE A STORY!!!!!!!

Be Your Own Kind of Beautiful

The Real Coco Mocho

MEMPHIS, TENNESSEE

THE REAL "COCO MOCHA"

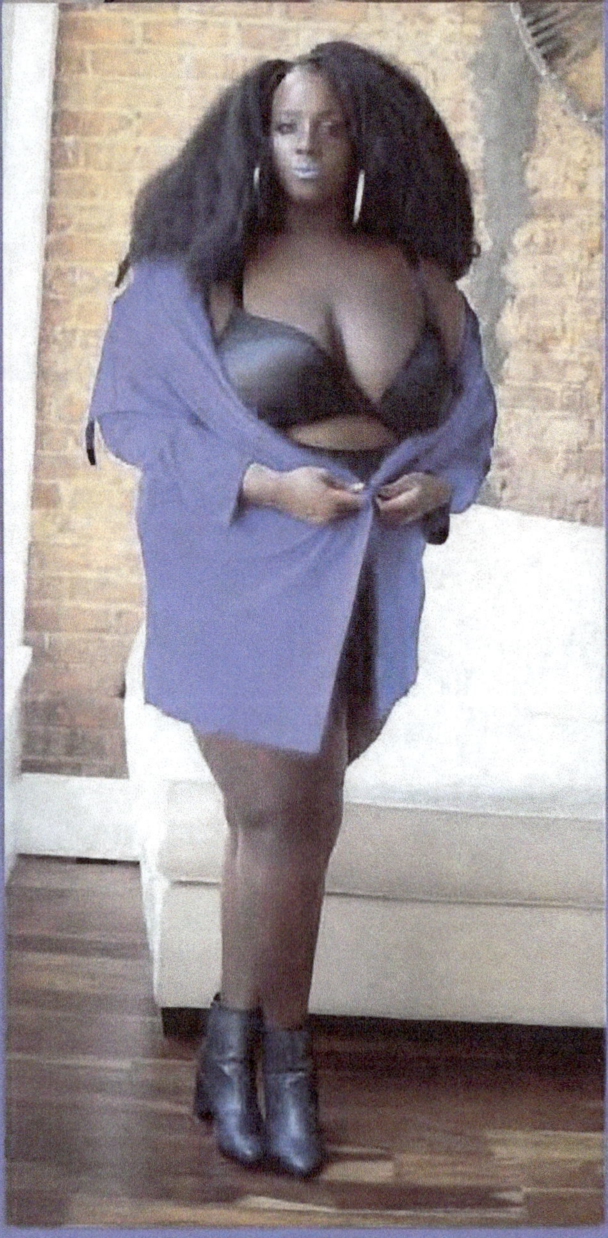

"CoCo Mocha"

MEMPHSIS, TENNESSE

Height 5'8
Dress Size
16/18

Choyce TV
NETFLIX
hulu
YouTube
amazon
sling
HBO GO
WATCH
PLEX
Size Fashions Shows & Interviews w
Plus Size Models
ChoyceTv.com
You Have a Choyce

Trina
"Brown
Suga"

Foxie Roxie
PHILADELPHIA, PA

"EVERY DAY, I WORK HARD TOWARDS MY GOALS. AS A SINGLE MOTHER & TEACHER, I ASPIRE TO BE MORE & TO DO MORE FOR MYSELF, FAMILY, AND COMMUNITY!"

Foxie Roxie
Philadelphia, PA
"Be your own kind of Beautiful!"
educator
model
singer
Dress Size: 14/16 Height: 5'10

MY BODY
IS
ART!

Rae Nicole
Baltimore,
Maryland

Dress size 14/16
Height 5'10

Courbee' Couture

Intimate Apparel

A Division of Jamila Jay Fashions

JAMILAJAYPLUSSIZE.com

Christa Cora

Christa Cora

GLEN RIDGE,
NEW JERSEY

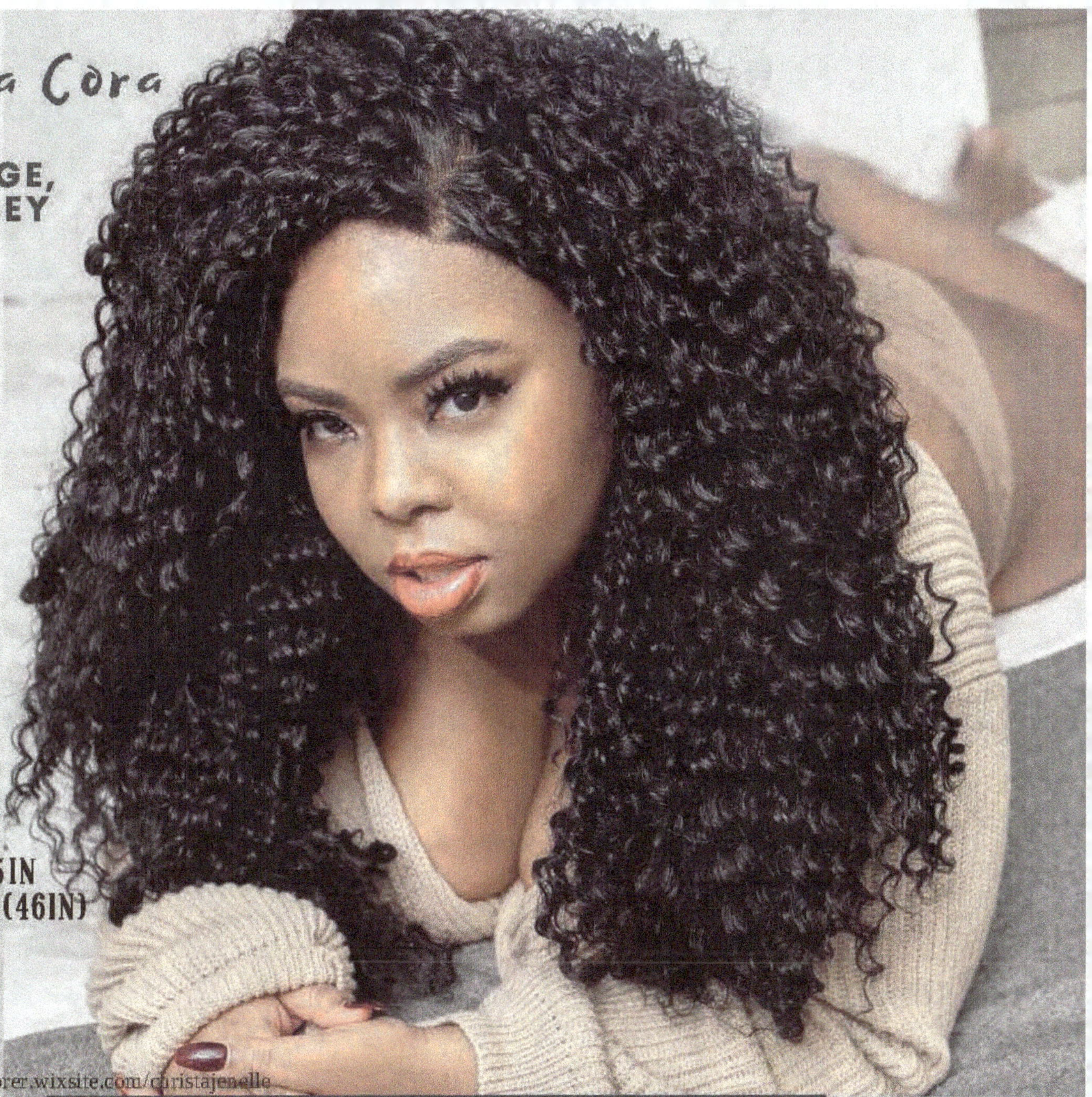

EIGHT: 5FT5IN
UST: 42DDD (46IN)
IPS: 46IN
AIST: 38IN
HOE: 8.5
ze: 16/18
ebsite: coratexplorer.wixsite.com/christajenelle

"JUST BE TRUE TO WHO YOU ARE, NO MATTER WHAT SIZE OR SHAPE YOU MIGHT BE!"

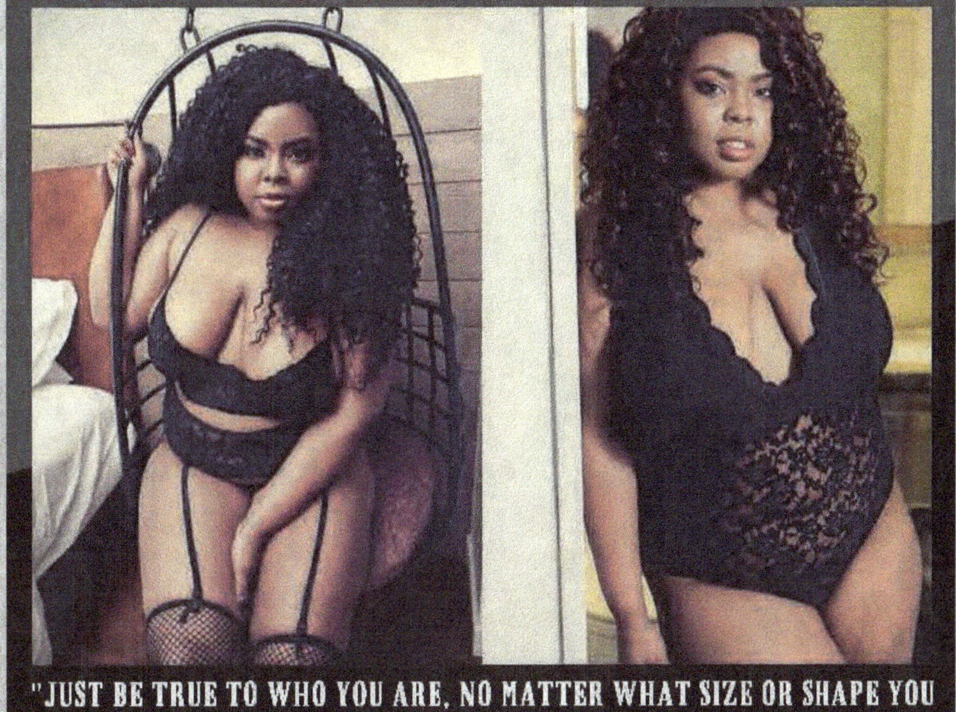

LADOM STYLEZZ
OAKLAND, CALIFORNIA

PHOTOGRAPHER
MKI PHOTOGRAPHER

"The Dream is Free, but the Hustle is Sold Separately."
La Dom

Height 5'5
Dress Size 14/16 or XL

JAMILAJAYPLUSSIZECASTING
Plus Size
CASTING
JAMILAJAYPlusSizeCasting.com
...NG AGENCY, PLUS SIZE FASHION WEEK, PAGEANTS, REALITY SHOWS, FASHION SHOWS, COMMERCIALS, TELEVISION FEATURES & EXTRA!
www.JAMILAJAYPLUSSIZECASTING.COM
JAMILAJAYPLUSSIZECASTING@GMAIL.COM

Renee Marie

Vallejo, California

My body is a Master Piece

SueWong McFadden, Durham, North Carolina

"ONE BREATH AT A TIME"

*written by
Author Karen Brown
Dickson*

Karen Dickson Brown has devoted her life to being compassionate and caring while spreading love and hope to those who cross her path.

Karen is a native of Stamford Connecticut, the child of Mr. Coleridge J. Dickson II and the late Patricia E. Dickson. Mrs. Brown Shared her parents with two sisters and one brother and later in life blessed with three younger siblings.

Mrs. Brown a former school teacher in Connecticut continues to hold a special place within her heart for all children. Serving as a lifetime advocate for abandoned, misplaced children and young adults has been very fulfilling.

She has found joy in assisting pregnant girls who were alone, displaced, giving support during labor & delivery, but most of all unconditional love and a lot of hugs. The numerous persons who have crossed

Mrs. Brown's path allowing her to mentor, assist with housing needs and teach basic home and life skills has in return blessed her tremendously.

Mrs. Brown has worked in the mental health field for over 20 years, the previous Executive Director of a DV/SA Agency, and Director of Development and Shelter Services within a local Homeless Program.

Mrs. Brown having received the Cata Purple Ribbon Award in 2015 from the Virginia Statewide Domestic Violence and Sexual Assault Action Alliance, which "honors one working specifically in the field of domestic violence for demonstrating exemplary commitment to restoring power and hope to victims who have experienced domestic violence through the provision of direct client services.

She, continues assisting those in need while thriving daily with the Lords assistance to reach and touch all who have yet to find their voice as they silently cry out for help.

Mrs. Brown has founded the ESIII "No Limits" Foundation after the loss of her middle child Eddie. ESIII is a mentoring program which provides support, love and guidance the EDDO (Educate, Decide, Develop, Overcome) way.

AUTHOR, MINISTER, & SURVIVOR

Mrs. Brown a Licensed Minister and Certified Life Coach has served within the Ministers Wives & Ministers Widows Association of the Wayland Blue Ridge Baptist Association, Virginia Chapter. Mrs. Brown is the First Lady of Pilgrim Baptist Church, Locust Grove VA; she adores her church family who has graciously and wholeheartedly accepted her into their hearts. She enjoys singing in the choir, serving as a deaconess, teaching Sunday school, and working within the women's ministry. She is married to the humble Pastor Garry M. Brown, mother of three sons she adores and Nona to five precious granddaughters. Mrs. Brown, Minister, Mentor, Motivator, Life Coach, Author (K.D.Brown) and so much more, lives daily by the Word with her favorite book in the bible being Proverbs as she strives for more wisdom each day..

Email: kydbrown@yahoo.com Website: www.gumroad.com/kydbrown
Facebook: Karen Dickson-Brown Instagram: kyd.brown Twitter: kyd_brown
Books available through Website (with autograph), Amazon & Barnes and Nobles.
Preaching, Speaking & Book Engagements Accepted
Books: 1. One Breath At A Time
2. Read-Breathe-Journal
3. Telling Our Story "Surviving & Thriving (Book collaboration with 4 others)
4. Breathing (coming soon)
Coming in 2021:
1. 3 Daily Devotional Books I was blessed join in on with woman from around the world
2. And so much more...